A Prayer of Hope

A Prayer of Hope
From Despair to Praise

Edna Robinson

XULON PRESS

Xulon Press
2301 Lucien Way #415
Maitland, FL 32751
407.339.4217
www.xulonpress.com

© 2018 by Edna Robinson

All rights reserved solely by the author. The author guarantees all contents are original and do not infringe upon the legal rights of any other person or work. No part of this book may be reproduced in any form without the permission of the author. The views expressed in this book are not necessarily those of the publisher.

Unless otherwise indicated, Scripture quotations taken from the King James Version (KJV) – *public domain*.

Edited by Xulon Press.

Printed in the United States of America.

ISBN-13: 978-1-54564-322-8

To God who gives hope through faith in Jesus Christ.

To those who struggle with adverse situations in life,
God's Word can provide hope when
discouragement overwhelms.

Table of Contents

Foreword ix

Losing A Loved One 1
A Prayer Of Hope 2
Restore My Soul 4
All Good Things Come Down From The Father 5
Every Good Gift 6
Great God. 7
Redeemer 8
Trust In God. 9
Trust In The Lord 10
One Day Of God 11
The Glorious Day 12
Glorious And Merciful. 13
Salvation 14
The Rock 15
The Rock of Salvation 16
Jesus! Amazing! 17
Walking On Water. 18
Stand Fast!. 19
Stand On The Word! 20
Grace 21
Grace And Truth. 22

The Way, The Walk, And The Word 23
The Way, The Truth, And The Life 24
The Way 25
The Path 26
Free 27
Free To Walk 28
Spiritual Walk 29
Wisdom! Our Sister 30
Wisdom 32
The Fungus 33
The House 35
Philosophies Of Humans (Satire Of The Foolish) . . 36
The Foolish 38

FOREWORD

HOPE

"Hope deferred makes the heart sick..." (Proverbs 13:12, KJV)

A Prayer of Hope is comprised of poems with scriptural verses of inspiration gain from God's Word to gives hope when discouraging situations overwhelms the mind and adversities trouble the soul. As Scripture encourages, *"with God all things are possible"* (Matthew 19:16; Mark 10:27).

A Prayer of Hope is also presented in a poem that explains a situation in which hope is deferred and causes an emptiness within the soul resulting from the inability to gain the desires of the heart. The void begins to flood the mind with negative emotions of bitterness, regret, and resentment. But, in the mist of the despairing thoughts, a memory sparks a prayer of hope to God, and the inspiration and instruction provided from God's Word renews the hope that was lost.

Hope is a longing for or a desire to achieve a goal, to overcome difficulties, or to change undesirable circumstances. Longing to obtain desires of the heart or hoping to accomplish goals are life endeavors. However, when longings are unfulfilled and things desired are unattainable, then expectations are cut off and the human spirit is brought low, causing the mind to become disconcerted. As the Bible informs, *"Hope deferred make the heart sick: but when the desire comes, it is a tree of life"* (Proverbs 13:12). As a tree transforms each Spring to mature and bring forth newness of life, God's Word proclaims, *"And be renewed in the spirit of your mind"* (Ephesians 4:23). Although adversities and discouragements unsettle the mind, God's Word, as a "tree of life," can rejuvenate the soul and lift the spirit to new heights of understanding to bring forth an expected end, *"Delight yourself in the LORD; and he shall give you the desires of your heart"* (Psalms 37:4)

A Prayer of Hope is filled with insightful, spiritual messages offered to inspire readers to renew hope in God's Word through faith in Jesus Christ, *"and be you transformed by the renewing of your mind, that you may prove what is that good, and acceptable, and perfect, will of God"* (Romans 12:2).

LOSING A LOVED ONE

Think back and remember when she was
full of life with so much expectation and
so much to live for.

Think back and remember the happy times
shared in her presence at family
gatherings and social outings.

Think back and remember the joy of her
laughter, the expressions on her face,
and the happiness in her smiles.

Think back and remember how depressing
it is to see a loved one suffer. Even the
thought of the pain she endured is heart-
rending and stressful.

Think back and remember the uncertainty
of her situation, the enormity of her
circumstances, and the inability to stop
the pain and change the course from
something so unthinkable as losing a
loved one.

Think back and remember: Truly, she will
be missed.

*In loving memory of my sister Pamela Alston, who died from
cancer in 1999.*

A Prayer Of Hope

In this dark and empty void, a swirl
of bad emotions form: anger, bitterness,
regret, and resentment flow in this dark
and empty void.

Rejection flood into, heartfelt loses as
hurtful memories filter through.

In despair! What shall I do?
In despair! What shall I do?

O' God of Hope!

Satan seeks to grab a hold to twist
my mind and take my soul.

Do not leave me all alone in this
dark and empty void!
Do not leave me all alone in this
dark and empty void!

Where is the hope that I once knew?

Memory sparks a prayer of hope that
lights the way and beckons me.
Get the Book! Get the Book!
Hope for me is in God's Book!

Shine forth Your light; fill up my mind,
and guide my soul to higher ground.

Fill up my mind, and save me now!
Fill up my mind, and save me now!

O' God of Hope!

Satan seeks to grab a hold to twist
my mind and take my soul.

Do not leave me all alone in this
dark and empty void!
Do not leave me all alone in this
dark and empty void!

Here is the hope renewed in You!

I have read Your Book! I have read
Your Book! Your words of Hope have
flood my soul!

Your words removed those swirling
forms, and the hope I had has been
restored; to a greater Hope than I
ever knew, and now my soul has been
renewed.

Praise to You! O' God of Hope!
Praise to You! O' God of Hope!

In loving memory of my sister Jean Foster, who struggled with depression before her death in 1986.

Restore My Soul

He restores my soul; he leads me in paths of righteousness for his name's sake (Psalms 23:3).

And now Lord, what wait I for? my hope is in thee (Psalms 39:7).

For we are saved by hope: but hope that is seen is not hope: for what a man sees, why does he yet hope for? (Romans 8:24)

All Good Things Come Down From The Father

All good things come down from the Father
of Lights. God's deep and spiritual things
give insight to the account of His Word
and the love that is confirmed to bring us
out of darkness into His marvelous light.

All good things come down from the Father
of Lights. God's deep and spiritual things
give insight to the glory of His Word
and goodness that is declared to guide
us out of despair into a joyful life.

All good things come down from the Father
of Lights. God's deep and spiritual things
give insight to the mystery of His Word
and the meanings that are revealed to lead
us from the path of wickedness onto His
path of righteousness.

All good things come down from the Father
of Lights. God's deep and spiritual things
give insight to the wisdom of His Word
and the knowledge that is transferred to awake
from spiritual blindness to walk in
His loving kindness.

All good things come down from the Father
of Lights.

EVERY GOOD GIFT

Every good gift and every perfect gift is from above, and comes down from the Father of lights, with whom is no variableness, neither shadow of turning (James 1:17).

But God has revealed them unto us by his Spirit for the Spirit searches all things, yes, the deep things of God (1 Corinthians 2:10).

GREAT GOD

Great God! Great God Almighty!
Lord, Everlasting Lord, ever reigning
in our souls;

Reign Truth, reign Peace, reign Love,
reign Joy upon our world, throughout
our land.

Hear our prayer; heal our land;
Save our lives; save our souls;

Hear our plead; hear our cry;
Change our hearts; change our lives.

Great God! Great God Almighty!
Lord, Everlasting Lord, ever reigning
in our souls.

Reign Truth, reign Peace, reign Love,
reign Joy; upon our world, throughout
our land.

Redeemer

For their redeemer is mighty; he shall plead their cause with thee (Proverbs 23:11).

Trust In God

Trust in God from whom all blessings
flow. Praise Father, Son, and Holy Ghost.

Have faith that God is Lord of all.
Have confidence that He will provide
good things that are required. Follow
the instructions of the wise.

Trust in God from whom all blessings
flow. Praise Father, Son, and Holy Ghost.

Stand firm on His Word and believe.
Ask and God's Promises you shall receive.
Seek and His blessings will come.

Trust in God from whom all blessings
flow. Praise Father, Son, and Holy Ghost.

Trust In The Lord

Trust in the Lord with all thine heart; and lean not unto thine own understanding. In all your ways acknowledge him, and he shall direct your paths (Proverbs 3:5-6).

The LORD is good, a stronghold in the day of trouble; and he knows them that trust in him (Nahum 1:7).

Charge them that are rich in this world, that they be not high minded, nor trust in uncertain riches, but in the living God, who gives us richly all things to enjoy; that they do good, that they be rich in good works, ready to distribute, willing to communicate; laying up in store for themselves a good foundation against the time to come, that they may lay hold on eternal life (1 Timothy 6:17-19).

ONE DAY OF GOD

A new day dawning,
a new millennium,
one-thousand years;
One Day of God.

Righteousness revealing,
His Spirit pouring out,
Showing us His Way.

Illuminating light,
Shining forth unto,
the perfect Day;
The Day of our Lord.

Coming in power, majesty,
and glory of God.

A new day dawning,
a new millennium,
one-thousand years;
One Day of God.

THE GLORIOUS DAY

And he laid hold on the dragon, that old serpent, which is the Devil, and Satan, and bound him a thousand years, And cast him into the bottomless pit, and shut him up, and set a seal upon him, that he should deceive the nations no more, till the thousand years should be fulfilled... (Revelation 20:2-3)

When Satan was cast out of heaven and came into the earth, he planned to deceive the minds of God's human creation. His plan was fulfilled and mankind fell into spiritual deception through Satan's evil influences. But, as the Bible informs, there will be a Glorious Day, as the LORD God promised, and Satan will not be able to deceive the nations, the people anymore for a thousand years or however long God the Father commands. What a Glorious Day that will be!

Glorious And Merciful

Glorious Father, Merciful Lord;
Sent us Love from heaven above,
Reigned down Truth throughout
our land, and delivered us from
Satan's hands.

SALVATION

The LORD lives; and blessed be my rock; and exalted be the God of the rock of my salvation (2 Samuel 22:47).

THE ROCK

Lead me to the Rock of my Salvation;
Guide me with Your Holy Spirit;
Fill me with Your Word of Wisdom;
Show me Your Righteous Way that leads
me to the Rock of my Salvation.

The Rock of Salvation

Jesus was born in an era of human history where the influence of evil prevailed in the minds of many people living throughout the Roman Empire, as evident from Herod's order to kill children, in all Bethlehem and the coastal areas, ages two years and under (Matthew 2:16), and the torturous ways accomplished to destroy the body of Jesus Christ (Mark 15:15-20). Although, according to scripture, Jesus Christ could have put an end to all who had condemned Him to death, which He said, *"Think you that I cannot now pray to my Father, and he shall presently give me more than twelve legions of angels?"* (Matthew 26:53) However, His death had a far greater spiritual purpose than most people imagine. Therefore, although Jesus Christ suffered an agonizing and horrific death, which has been misunderstood throughout the ages, His death brought salvation and life to all who believe.

Jesus Christ was conceived by the Holy Spirit of God (Luke 1:35), and born into the world, specifically as the fulfillment of God's plan of Salvation to save His human creation. God stepped down from His glorious throne to become the Sacrificial Lamb required to cover the sins of His human creation. God provided the first sacrifice to cover the sinful nature of mankind (Genesis 3:20). Then, God provided Himself as the last sacrifice to save His human creation, Jesus Christ—fully God and fully man.

JESUS! AMAZING!

Truly amazing, Jesus amazing;
Truly amazing our King.

He is Mary's baby, full of Grace,
Love, and Truth.

He is our Savior who died on the
cross, arose, and lived again.

He is our Lord who ascended to
heaven and gave gifts to men.

He is our King who sits on the
right hand of God and judge the
nations. Yes, He judge the nations.

Truly amazing, Jesus amazing;
Truly amazing is our King.

He is the Lord of lords,
The King of kings, and
The Bright and Morning Star.

He is the Rock of Ages,
The Chief Cornerstone, and
The Blessed Redeemer who saves us.

Truly amazing, Jesus amazing;
Truly amazing is our King.

He is truly amazing!

WALKING ON WATER

And in the fourth watch of the night Jesus went unto them walking on the sea. And when the disciples saw him walking on the sea, they were troubled, saying, It is a spirit; and they cried out for fear (Matthew 14:25-26).

And Peter answered and said, Lord, if it be you, bid me come unto you on the water. And he said, Come. And when Peter was come down out of the ship, he walked on the water, to go to Jesus. But when he saw the wind boisterous, he was afraid, and beginning to sink, he cried, saying, Lord, save me. And immediately Jesus stretched forth his hand and caught him, and said unto him, O you of little faith, wherefore did you doubt? (Matthew 14:28-31)

STAND FAST!

Stand fast!
Stand fast, therefore in Liberty
that makes us free.

Now, Lord is that Spirit: and
Where the Spirit of the Lord is,
There is Liberty.

Christ has made us free!
We're free indeed!

We're created by God!
We're redeemed by the Lord!
We're free indeed!

We're free to walk in God's perfect
Law of Liberty that makes us free.
We're free indeed!

Stand fast!
Stand fast, therefore, in Liberty.

Biblical quote italicized from 2 Corinthians 3:17.

Stand On The Word!

The works of his hands are verity and judgement; all his commandments are sure. They stand fast forever and ever, and are done in truth and uprightness (Psalms 111:7-8).

Stand fast therefore in liberty wherewith Christ has made us free, and be not entangled again with the yoke of bondage (Galatians 5:1)

Stand firm on the righteous Word of God and walk in the Way of the Lord Jesus Christ, guided by God's Holy Spirit.

GRACE

It is Jesus Christ who gave up His
life as a sacrifice:

To die for our sins, then
lived again, and gave gifts
to men.

It is Jesus Christ who gave up His
life as a sacrifice:

To release our thoughts from Satan's sway.
We are no longer bound to his wicked ways.
Our souls set free from Satan's hold.
So, we may know God's Way to go.

It is Jesus Christ who gave up His
life as a sacrifice:

To direct our path to God's righteous
plan and guide us to God's promises.

It is Jesus Christ!

GRACE AND TRUTH

For the law was given by Moses, but grace and truth came by Jesus Christ (John 1:17).

For by grace are you saved through faith; and that not of yourselves: it is the gift of God (Ephesians 2:8).

But unto every one of us is given grace according to the measure of the gift of Christ (Ephesians 4:7).

The Way, The Walk, and The Word

The way is the walk of life through the Word
that paid a great price to bring salvation to
mankind's life.

God Brought Forth His Word! Though Satan
fulfilled his plan and deceived the soul of
man, to oppose what God commanded;

God Brought Forth His Word! Though Satan
toiled throughout the ages to destroy
God's human creation;

God Brought Forth His Word! Through that
which God conceived for mankind to receive
to end what Satan had schemed.

The way is the walk of life through the Word that
paid a great price and became precious for
mankind's life.

Jesus Christ is the Word brought forth to
show the Way to Walk in God's plan for life.

THE WAY, THE TRUTH, AND THE LIFE

Jesus said unto him, I am the way, the truth, and the life: no man comes unto the Father, but by me (John 14:6, KJV).

THE WAY

In the peace and quietness,
tranquil in the solitude, a
whisper of a still small voice
beckons me to come:
Up the narrow path it says;
Up the narrow path.

Keep your footsteps straight.
Do not deviate; not to the right,
nor to the left.
Keep your footsteps straight;
up the narrow path.

In the peace and quietness,
tranquil in the solitude,
God's Holy Spirit guides me
up the narrow path.

The Path

That you may walk in the way of good men, and keep the paths of the righteous (Proverbs 2:20).

But the path of the just is as the shining light, that shines more and more unto the perfect day (Proverbs 4:18).

Howbeit when he, the Spirit of truth is come, he will guide you into all truth... (John 16:13).

FREE

When we learn to believe; when we
learn to stand firm on words that
liberally serve:

To free our souls from erring woes,
to soar our spirits to new heights,
to seek a higher Way of life.

Ways of good and right and pure.
Ways of Truth to light our path.
Ways of God's higher plan.

When we learn to believe; when we
learn to stand firm on God's
infallible Word.

FREE TO WALK

If the Son therefore shall make you free, you shall be free indeed (John 8:36).

The knowledge of God and the deep things pertaining to God, which are revealed in the Bible, make us spiritually free. The Holy Spirit of God guides us to search out the hidden things of God to establish our lives on a firm foundation and walk in the way that reflects the true image of God.

Spiritual Walk

If we live in the Spirit, let us also walk in the Spirit (Galatians 5:25).

Your word is a lamp unto my feet, and a light unto my path (Psalms 119:105)

Let your light so shine before men, that they may see your good works, and glorify your Father which is in heaven (Matthew 5:16).

The Spiritual Walk is the Way of Life in Christ:

1. God is the author, and His Way characterizes the Walk of life for believers.
2. God has encouraged and instructed His Way since the beginning of creation.
3. God's Way is not grievous.
4. The Walk is confirmed throughout the Bible from the Old Testament to the New Testament.
5. The Walk is a reflection of God.
6. The Walk glorifies God and draws others to seek Him.
7. The Walk is a life established on the deep things of God.
8. The Way is a firm foundation for believers to live a life in Christ.
9. Jesus Christ is the Way that exemplified the Walk encouraged through the Word.

Wisdom! Our Sister

Wisdom is the principal thing.
Wisdom is our sister.
Wisdom cries out to us saying:

Awake! You simple minded siblings.
Awake, out of your sleep!

Hear my call, and seek me out.
Get wisdom! Get understanding too.

You cry out for joy;
You cry out for love;
You cry out for peace.
And seek the simpler things in life.

But, Wisdom is the principal thing.
Wisdom is our sister.
Wisdom cries out to us saying:

Awake! You simple minded siblings.
Awake, out of your sleep!

Hear my call and seek me out.
Get wisdom and get understanding too.

You cry out for justice;
You cry out for liberty;
You cry out for mercy;
And seek the simpler things in life.

But, Wisdom is the principal thing.
Wisdom is our sister.

Wisdom cries out to us saying:

Awake! You simple minded siblings.
Awake, out of your sleep!

Seek Wisdom from God. She is the
principal thing.

WISDOM

For the LORD gives wisdom: out of his mouth comes knowledge and understanding (Proverbs 2:6).

Does not wisdom cry? And understanding put forth her voice? She stands in the top of high places, by the way in the places of the paths. She cries at the gates, at the entry of the city at the coming in at the doors. Unto you, O men, I call; and my voice is to the sons of man. O you simple, understand wisdom: and you fools, be you of an understanding heart (Proverbs 8:1-5).

If any of you lack wisdom, let him ask of God, that gives to all men liberally, and upbraids not; and it shall be given him (James 1:5).

THE FUNGUS

A family moved into their new home;
relatives and friends welcomed them in.
They had accomplished their goal;
they bought their dream home.

It had been inspected.
It had passed the test.
So, no one suspected.

There was a small crack, just in
the back along the outside wall.
Dampness settled and moisture
soaked all during the fall.

The fungus grew from the dew and
seeped in between the walls; and as it
grew, it spread right through to the
vents in the hall.

It had been inspected.
It had passed the test.
So, no one suspected.

The chill in the air gave a sudden
reminder that winter was settling in.
The family adjusted; their thermostat
set, prepared for the cold days ahead.

The warmth filtered through the open
vents and into the air the fungus went.

THE FUNGUS

It had been inspected;
It had passed the test.
So, no one suspected.

A few sneezes, some stuffy noses,
coughs that continued to linger;
A plague of sore throats and
headaches too.

Is it the flu? It must be a change in
the weather.

But, it had been inspected.
It had passed the test.
So, no one suspected.

Their dream home is now infested.

The House

And he that owns the house shall come and tell the priest, saying, It seems to me there is as it were a plague in the house; then the priest shall command that they empty the house, before the priest go into it to see the plague, that all that is in the house be not made unclean: and afterward the priest shall go into to see the house: and he shall look on the plague, and behold, if the plague be in the walls of the house with hollow strakes, greenish or reddish, which in sight are lower than the wall; then the priest shall go out of the house to the door of the house, and shut up the house seven days...then the priest shall come and look, and behold, if the plague be spread in the house, it is a fretting leprosy in the house: it is unclean (Leviticus 14:34-44).

PHILOSOPHIES OF HUMANS
(SATIRE OF THE FOOLISH)

Many have said from their heart of hearts (their conscience),
There is no God!

Let's search the stars!
Men are from Mars!
Women are from Venus!
But, Venus was too hot for men; and, Mars
was too cold and dry for women.
So, Earth turned out just right for them.

Many have said from their heart of hearts (their conscience),
There is no God!

The universe started with a big bang!
Wonder where are all the other humans?
The planets should be full, overpopulated by now!
Could they have all been genetically engineered wrong?

Many have said from their heart of hearts (their conscience),
There is no God!

Humans evolved from apes!
Humans evolved from the sea!
Wonder why the others didn't evolve?
Wonder if it had something to do with that meteor?
You know, the one that wiped out the dinosaurs
billions of years ago.

Philosophies Of Humans (Satire Of The Foolish)

Many have said from their heart of hearts (their conscience),
There is no God!

There is no right! There is no wrong!
Wonder why the leaders of the nations spend so much
money on defense?
Could it be that someone might cause harm?
Is this right? Or, is this wrong?
Wonder what it would be called if there is no right;
if there is no wrong?

Many have said from their heart of hearts (their conscience),
The foolish philosophies of humans.

The Foolish

The fool has said in his heart, There is no God. They are corrupt… (Psalms 14:1).

Beware least any man spoil you through philosophy and vain deceit, after the tradition of men, after the rudiments of the world, and not after Christ (Colossians 2:8).

CPSIA information can be obtained
at www.ICGtesting.com
Printed in the USA
BVHW09s0123280818
525775BV00007B/171/P